The Green-Eyed Goblin

What to do about jealousy – for all children including those on the Autism Spectrum

K.I. Al-Ghani

Illustrated by Haitham Al-Ghani

Jessica Kingsley *Publishers*
London and Philadelphia

First published in 2017
by Jessica Kingsley Publishers
73 Collier Street
London N1 9BE, UK
and
400 Market Street, Suite 400
Philadelphia, PA 19106, USA

www.jkp.com

Copyright © K.I. Al-Ghani 2017
Illustrations copyright © Haitham Al-Ghani 2017
Cover illustration by Haitham Al-Ghani

All rights reserved. No part of this publication may be reproduced in any material form (including photocopying, storing in any medium by electronic means or transmitting) without the written permission of the copyright owner except in accordance with the provisions of the law or under terms of a licence issued in the UK by the Copyright Licensing Agency Ltd. www.cla.co.uk or in overseas territories by the relevant reproduction rights organisation, for details see www.ifrro.org. Applications for the copyright owner's written permission to reproduce any part of this publication should be addressed to the publisher.

Warning: The doing of an unauthorised act in relation to a copyright work may result in both a civil claim for damages and criminal prosecution.

Library of Congress Cataloging in Publication Data
A CIP catalog record for this book is available from the Library of Congress

British Library Cataloguing in Publication Data
A CIP catalogue record for this book is available from the British Library

ISBN 978 1 78592 091 2
eISBN 978 1 78450 352 9

Printed and bound in China

This book is dedicated to
the memory of a dear husband and devoted
father, Ahmed Mohammed Al-Ghani

Introduction

Of all human emotions, jealousy has to be the most negative, the most destructive and the most difficult to control and conquer. Everyone – young and old, typical and atypical – has been visited by the Green-Eyed Goblin.

His effect on our psyche is unmistakable – a growing feeling of unhappiness and discontent descends, then the green mist exuded by the Green-Eyed Goblin begins to thicken and cloud our judgement. If we succumb to his poison, he can define how we feel about ourselves and how much happiness we can enjoy in life.

The Green-Eyed Goblin reminds us of something we don't have or are in danger of losing. This could be success, a special relationship, a talent or, more simplistically, the latest car, telephone or pair of shoes.

The Green-Eyed Goblin may awaken when we have something dear and become increasingly concerned by the threat of losing it. The "it" could be the love or admiration of a mother, father, husband, wife, friend, boyfriend, girlfriend or work colleague. He arises from our fear of comparison and can make us feel like a lesser person, and so we begin to think obsessively about our imperfections or shortcomings. This can then lead to a loss of self-esteem, and general unhappiness.

In children, the Green-Eyed Goblin can quickly turn into anger and hatred; in adults, he may manifest as an overwhelming sense of suspicion. In extreme cases, if left unchecked, it may foster a desire for retribution. This can change the Green-Eyed Goblin into a malevolent enemy, bent on revenge.

It is not hard to see how the Green-Eyed Goblin can influence children when they begin to feel rejected or not good enough. How often has he been awoken by that most damaging of phrases, "If only you could be more like…"?

In the emotionally immature world of the young person with Asperger Syndrome, jealousy can be both debilitating and damaging. It is so important to be able to recognize this emotion and learn how to control it.

One key difference between typical children and those on the Autism Spectrum is their ability (or inability) to talk about emotions. This is known as Alexithymia.

I suppose some might ask, "Do people with Autism experience and understand jealousy?"

Jealousy is an emotion that requires a relationship with others. This is well within the capacity of most children on the spectrum. It could be argued that showing jealousy is actually a good thing, since it means the child is developing a connectedness with other people. It has been suggested that experiencing jealousy may be a better indicator of where a child lies on the spectrum. Experiencing this emotion means the child has the capacity to establish secure attachments and develop friendships. The way that children with AS understand and reflect on this emotion may be somewhat distorted, but the experience will be real.

Getting a firm grip on the Green-Eyed Goblin before he can cause feelings of inferiority, outrage or betrayal is the key to improving happiness and contentment in life.

Deep inside everyone, a little goblin lies sleeping.

When he is sleeping, his eyes are a cool shade of blue, his nose is a cute little button and his breath is as fresh and sweet as a daisy.

However, should this little fellow be woken, his eyes turn from cool blue to emerald green.

His cute little nose begins to grow and grow and his breath becomes a smelly, green mist.

Sometimes, when fully awake, that little goblin's green breath comes snorting down his, by now, enormous nose.

So what is it that makes this adorable little goblin
wake up and become so hideous?

Well, it is something called **JEALOUSY**.

Jealousy is a very uncomfortable feeling we can all get when we see
someone getting something we would quite like to have ourselves.

It could be a new toy or computer game, better marks in
a test or a special prize from your favourite teacher.

We can also feel jealous when a person we like or love seems to like or love someone else more than us.

It could be due to the arrival of a new baby, with everyone fussing over it and forgetting all about us.

It could be the birthday of a brother or sister, when they get all the attention and lots of new toys.

It could be a new person in the class who makes friends with our very best friend, making us feel left out.

That Green-Eyed Goblin ALWAYS wakes up from his contented sleep when he hears the words,

"AAAW! I wish I had that!"

or,

"Hey, that's not fair!"

The Green-Eyed Goblin wakes up so grumpy
that he can make us feel bad inside.

He just loves to grumble and complain.

He might even tell us to do something mean or nasty.

It is important to put the Green-Eyed Goblin back to a peaceful sleep before we do something we might regret.

This is the story of a little boy called Theo, who woke up his Green-Eyed Goblin…

Early one Saturday morning, Theo woke up to the sound of his granny's voice downstairs.

He jumped out of bed and, as he put on his slippers, he thought it would be fun to sneak up on Granny and surprise her.

As he got near the bottom of the stairs he could see Granny sitting on the sofa with her arm around his sister, Jodie.

"AAAW, that's not fair!" he said to himself, "I wanted to see Granny first!"

Theo felt a funny sensation in his tummy. He had woken up the Green-Eyed Goblin.

The Green-Eyed Goblin had woken from a deep and pleasant sleep and blinked his blue eyes to see what was going on.

Theo crept closer to the sitting room and heard Granny say, "Now, my darling Jodie, what would you like for your birthday next week?"

Theo began to feel funny. The Green-Eyed Goblin was now fully awake and his cool blue eyes had turned to a bright emerald green. His cute little nose began to grow and grow.

Theo hid to the side of the door to listen what Jodie would say.

"Well, Granny," said Jodie, "I would really love a scooter."

The Green-Eyed Goblin began to snort a green,
smelly mist down his enormous nose.

Theo went into a rage and burst into the sitting room.

"**NO! NO! NO!**" screamed Theo. "That's not fair! **I want** a scooter! Jodie's just copying me!"

He lunged at Jodie and pulled her hair.

The Green-Eyed Goblin's breath was coming thick and fast.

Mum came running in to see what all the fuss was about. She grabbed Theo and took him upstairs.

Jodie was crying and poor Granny had to console her. She had never seen her grandson behave so badly before.

Theo was crying, too. Mum sat him down on the bed.

"Now tell me," said Mum calmly, "whatever is the matter?"

Between sobs, Theo said, "Granny loves Jodie better than me and she is going to get her a scooter for her birthday next week. I told Jodie that I wanted a scooter. She is just a mean old copycat. I hate her!"

The Green-Eyed Goblin was smiling and his green eyes twinkled with delight at the mischief he had made.

When Theo had finally calmed down, Mum
gave him a glass of water with a straw.

"You just woke up the Green-Eyed Goblin…" Mum said mysteriously.

Theo's eyes grew wide. "What Green-Eyed Goblin?" he asked
curiously.

"He is a sweet little goblin that sleeps happily
inside us, until," Mum said, "he hears someone say
'Hey, that's not fair!' or 'I wish I had that!'"

"I think everyone loves Jodie better than me," said Theo
sadly. "Sometimes I don't like her very much and then
something inside me makes me do mean things."

"Oh, that will be the Green-Eyed Goblin all right," continued Mum as she snuggled up to Theo. "He can get very mean when he thinks someone is getting more love and attention than him! I am going to have a little think and see if we can't do something to protect ourselves from that little goblin," she said with a smile.

"Now let's put Goblin back to sleep, shall we?" said Mum.
"Hold up your fingers and imagine they are ten candles. Take deep breaths and blow out those candles one by one."

The next day, when Theo got back from school, he found a small pop-up tent in his bedroom.

Mum told him that they were going to put some things in the tent to help him put the Green-Eyed Goblin back to sleep, should he wake up again.

"When you are inside this tent, the green mist made by the goblin cannot get to you," she said, reassuringly.

Theo was baffled. "What green mist?" he asked.

"Well, when the Green-Eyed Goblin gets mad, his nose grows and grows and his breath becomes smelly and green. This green mist comes down his huge nose and stops us from seeing things properly," Mum explained. "The more he makes, the less we can see straight. We begin to think we just aren't good enough and then we can turn mean and spiteful."

Theo remembered feeling just like that.

"Now," said Mum, matter-of-factly, "everyone feels like this sometimes. The feeling is called JEALOUSY, so we need to learn how to protect ourselves from the Green-Eyed Goblin, should he wake up, otherwise he can get us into real trouble and make us feel very unhappy and miserable.

First we are going to make something to remind us how special and lucky we are," said Mum.

She held up a large piece of white cardboard with a line drawn down the middle. On one half it said "favourite people" and on the other half it said "favourite things."

On the favourite people side, Theo put: Mum, Dad, Granny, Grandad, Jodie, Leon (his best friend), Mrs Linfield (his favourite teacher) and Rumble (his rabbit!).

On the favourite things side, he put: construction bricks; his toolbox, hardhat and lunch box; his dinosaur collection; his teddy, Somerset; all his video games and his collection of rocks.

"Now, tell me what makes Jodie a good sister," Mum went on.

"Well," Theo said, thoughtfully, "she is kind and helps me with my school work. If I get scared at night, she lets me sleep in her bed. And she taught me how to swim."

Mum wrote everything Theo loved about Jodie on special pink labels.

"Now tell me, what makes *you* a good brother?" asked Mum.

"Well, I can dress myself, fasten my shoes and make my bed, all by myself," said Theo proudly.

"I help Jodie to tidy her room. She is really messy… I tell her funny stories to make her laugh and I draw pictures for her," Theo went on, without stopping for breath.

Soon they had a whole heap of blue labels that mentioned all Theo's good qualities.

"If the Green-Eyed Goblin should wake up," said Mum, "go inside the tent. You will find a torch and your water bottle. I want you to take some really deep breaths and blow out each finger. Then drink some water and, using the torch, read all the labels."

"Next," continued Mum, "I want you to look at the list of favourite things. If the Green-Eyed Goblin is jealous of something like a new toy, think about what you could cross off your favourite things list so you can add the toy instead.

If the Green-Eyed Goblin is complaining because it seems like someone else is getting all the love and attention, I want you to think about crossing that person off your favourite people list and putting the Green-Eyed Goblin instead."

Mum and Theo practised going in the tent when the Green-Eyed Goblin was sound asleep, to be ready for him should he wake up.

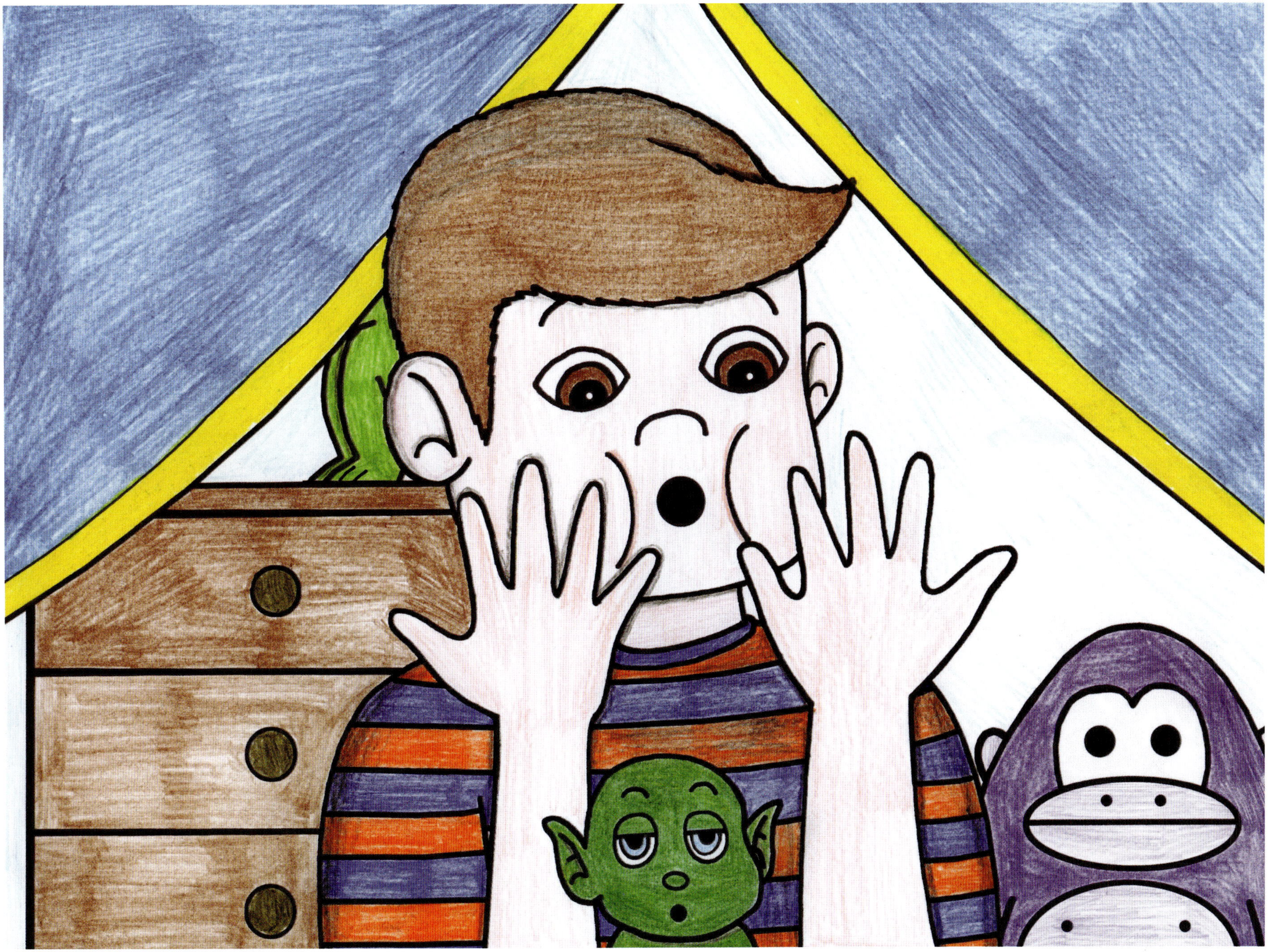

The next day, Theo went into the kitchen to find Jodie and Mum writing party invitations. On the table was a beautiful princess birthday cake that Granny had made.

Theo felt that funny feeling in his tummy again and he shouted,

"I wish it was my birthday! It's not fair! I want a scooter like Jodie!"

"Quick," said Mum, "to the tent!"

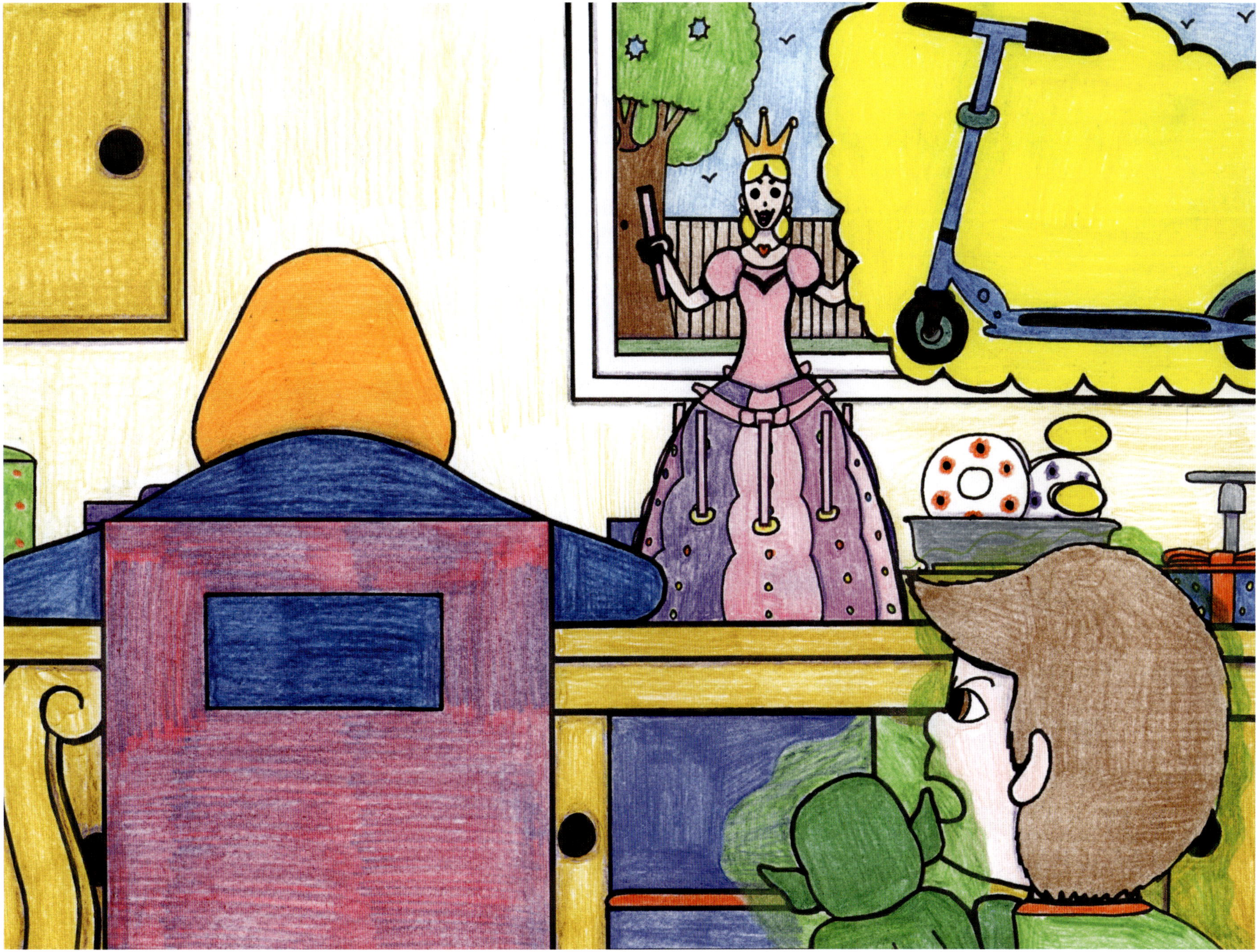

In the tent Theo took some deep breaths and blew out his candle fingers. Then he took sips of water through a straw. He read the labels and looked at his list of favourite things. He found that he didn't want to cross anything off his list because he liked everything too much.

Mum popped her head into the tent and Theo told her he didn't want to cross anything off his list.

"Okay," said Mum, wisely, "so maybe you can get the scooter when it is your birthday."

Theo thought that was a good idea and he didn't feel mad with Jodie anymore.

FAVOURITE THINGS:
• CONSTRUCTION BRICKS
• TOOL BOX
• HARD HAT
• LUNCH BOX
FAVOURITE PEOPLE:
• MUM
• DAD
• GRANNY
• GRANDAD

Two days before the party, Mum gave Theo lots of jobs to help with the party plans.

He drew pictures of birthday cakes and balloons on the invitations. He helped to wrap some of Jodie's presents. He helped Mum to make a list of favourite party foods. He even suggested a fancy dress party so that he could come as a construction worker and have a clipboard with the list of party games and events on it. Jodie loved that idea and so they added the words "fancy dress" in front of the word "party" on the invitations.

PARTY LIST
• INVITATIONS
• DECORATIONS
AKE
• FOOD
• PARTY GAMES
• GOODIES
LOUR
MUSTARD
KETCHUP
BREA
To Julie,

On the day of the party, Theo felt important in his contstruction worker's costume. As he walked downstairs he saw Grandad giving Jodie a big hug.

"I wish it was my birthday," Theo said under his breath. *"Grandad loves Jodie more than me!"*

Suddenly, Theo thought of the Green-Eyed Goblin and he rushed up to his tent. He took some deep breaths and blew out his candle fingers and sipped some water. Then, after reading the labels, he looked at the list of his favourite people. He knew that Grandad loved him just as much as Jodie really so he didn't want to cross him off his list. Instead of crossing Grandad off the list, he told the Green-Eyed Goblin to get lost!

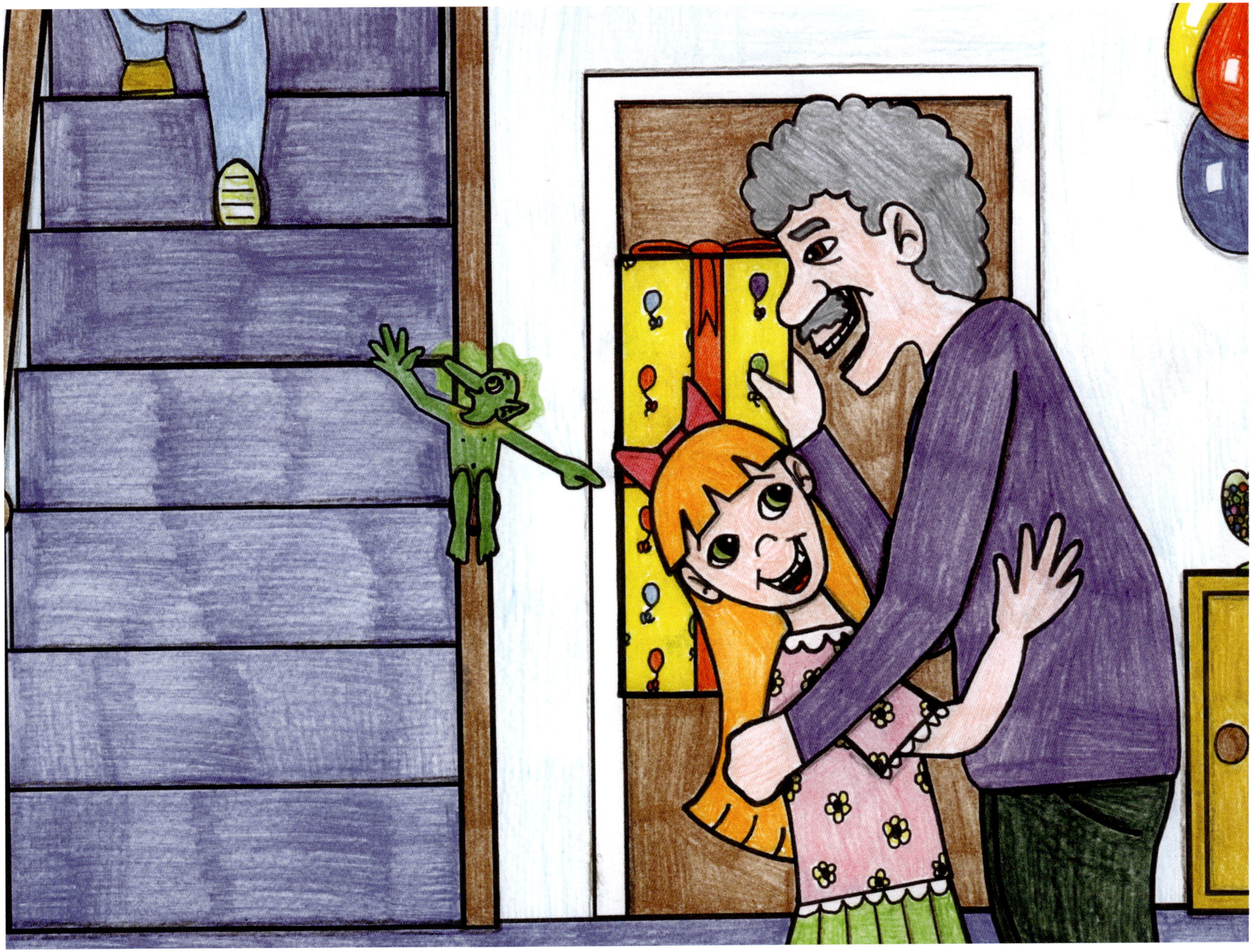

Theo left the tent feeling sure that the Green-Eyed Goblin was now fast asleep. However, as he reached the bottom stair, Jodie came scooting by on her new scooter.

The Green-Eyed Goblin jumped up and Theo was about to run back up to the safety of his tent, when one of the children shouted.

"Hey, look at Theo! AAAW! I wish I had a hard hat and tools – I knew this monkey costume was rubbish!"

Theo smiled broadly – it seemed like someone else had just woken up their Green-Eyed Goblin.

Theo joined the guests as they admired his costume and clipboard. Jodie said it was her best birthday ever.

Theo would often wake up that mean Green-Eyed Goblin, but now he knew just what to do to stop himself from being mean too.

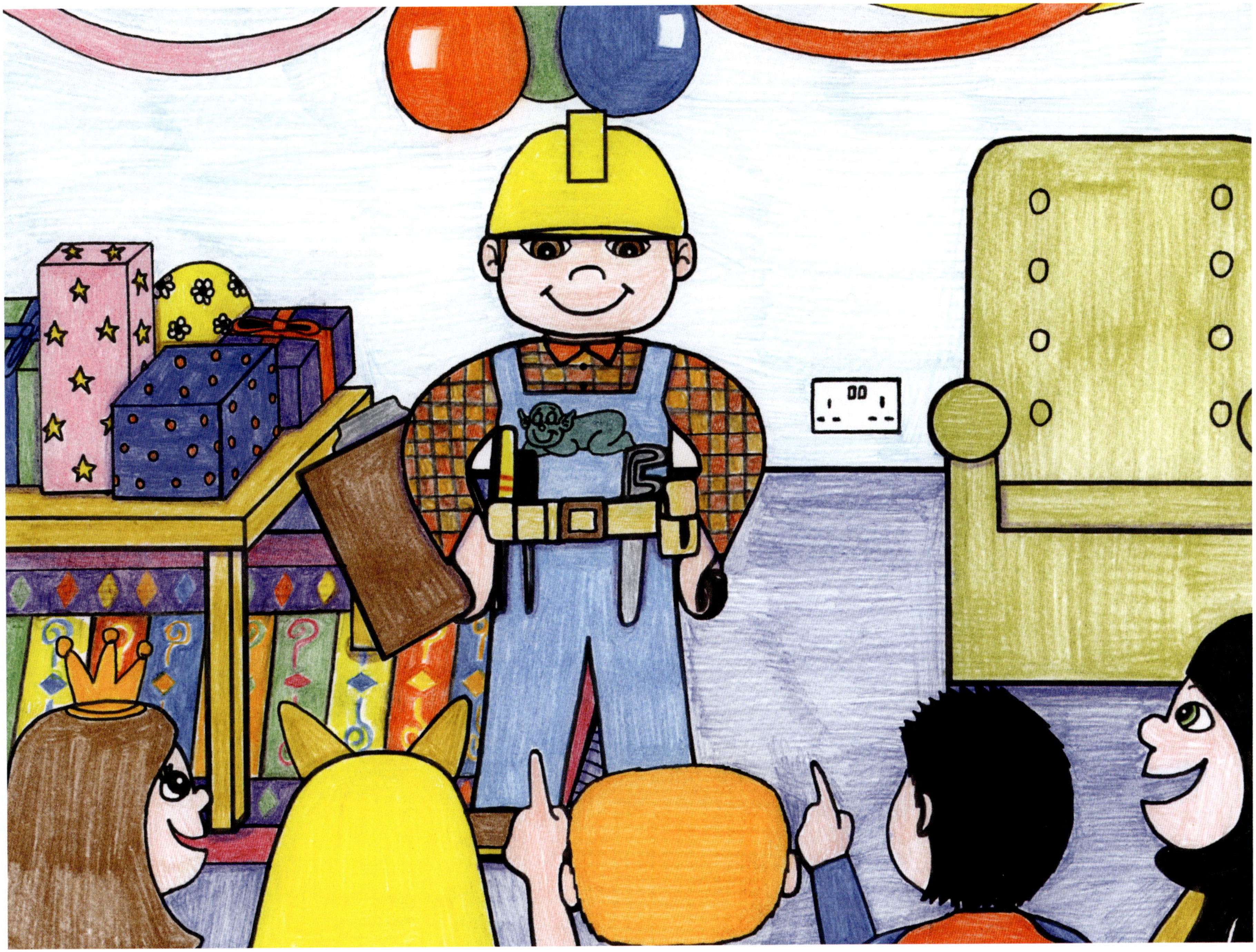

The Last Word

It is not hard to understand what it is that every child (indeed, every human being) needs. It is the 3 As: Attention, Affection and Approval.

Anyone involved in the well-being of children should ensure that every child gets a good measure of these three vital ingredients to develop self-esteem. Try these ideas:

- Open up a "Self-Esteem Bank Account" and ensure you make regular deposits. Show children what you value about them. I know it is difficult when children misbehave, but we must learn to criticize the action and not the person. Saying "I can see you are finding it difficult to… How can I help?" is a good place to start.

- Resist the temptation to make comparisons. Ditch that damaging phrase, "If only you could be more like…"

- Never compare – stress uniqueness and individuality. Give them the mantras:

    "Everyone is important; everyone is special, only I know how to be me."

    "It is nice to be important, but it is important to be nice."

- Always show pride in genuine accomplishments, for example saying sorry, controlling a fit of temper, being thoughtful and kind.

- Teachers could have a compliment chair, in which the children take turns to sit while others pay them a compliment using one of these four areas: skills, successes, personality and possessions.

- Get children to make lists of the important people and things in their life. Use this list when they become jealous and ask them to choose which one they would give away to get what they envy. Hopefully, they won't want to eliminate anything from that list! This is the way to get children to count their own blessings and *not* focus on someone else's. I used labels in the story but you could replace these with photographs – especially for younger children and children with Autism.

- Tend to your own self-esteem – remember, children learn by example. It seems futile to try to teach children how to cope with envy and jealousy if we display these emotions overtly ourselves.

- Involve children in the care of younger siblings and make sure you praise them for acts of kindness, especially when they're spontaneous.

- Plan ahead. If you know a birthday is coming up, think about the other siblings as well as the birthday boy or girl. They could help to wrap the gifts, send out the invitations, choose the cake, make the food, set the table or give out the party treats. Helping them to feel important won't take anything away from the birthday celebrant. This is especially important for children with ASD. They will also need to know, in advance, exactly what is going to happen for the birthday if they are not to be overwhelmed and possibly made jealous of the whole birthday experience.

- Many children with ASD find parties difficult. The noise, the unpredictability of other children and having people in the house can be very stressful. Making a checklist or visual timetable of events will help to show the child that soon everything will be back to normal. You may want to give the child some ear defenders or an iPod to help with the noise. A clipboard with a list of jobs the child could do will help them to feel more involved and in control.

- Ensure all children have a calendar with photos of upcoming birthdays or other important events – especially the birth of a sibling. Being involved in special projects linked to events on the calendar is immensely motivating and provides many opportunities to make deposits in the "Self-Esteem Bank."

- Teach children the importance of deep breathing. Use bubbles or a harmonica to encourage this in younger children. Learning to play a woodwind instrument is an excellent way to encourage deep breathing in older children.

- Help younger children and those with Autism to compile a scrapbook filled with their favourite people and things – this makes for soothing reading any time emotions run too high.

These strategies won't stop that Green-Eyed Goblin from waking up, but they may help to put him back to sleep.